The Open Door

poems by

Ruth Smullin

Finishing Line Press
Georgetown, Kentucky

The Open Door

In loving memory of Frank Smullin and of my parents.

For my daughters.

Copyright © 2020 by Ruth Smullin
ISBN 978-1-64662-356-3 First Edition
All rights reserved under International and Pan-American Copyright Conventions. No part of this book may be reproduced in any manner whatsoever without written permission from the publisher, except in the case of brief quotations embodied in critical articles and reviews.

ACKNOWLEDGMENTS

The author would like to thank the editors of the following journals, where these poems first appeared, sometimes in earlier versions.

Bagelbards Anthologies: Monument Beach, Moving the Peonies, Not Like This My Father, The Open Door
Constellations: Miriam's Blue Suit, Wax
Crucible: Lucky (Winner of the Sam Ragan Prize)
Ibbetson Street: Bonnard's Painting: Nude in the Bath and Small Dog, Brushing Hair, Lost
Naugatuck River Review: Yellow (nominated for a Pushcart Prize)
Plainsongs: Old Letters
Sow's Ear Poetry Review: Pomegranate, Raspberries
The Aurorean: Raspberry Patch in Winter

Publisher: Leah Huete de Maines
Editor: Christen Kincaid
Cover Art: *Dining Room in the Country*, Pierre Bonnard, 1913
Author Photo: Adnan Adam Onart
Cover Design: Elizabeth Maines McCleavy

Order online: www.finishinglinepress.com
also available on amazon.com

Author inquiries and mail orders:
Finishing Line Press
P. O. Box 1626
Georgetown, Kentucky 40324
U. S. A.

Table of Contents

Yellow 1

The Open Door 2

Monument Beach 3

Class Photo 4

My Portion 6

Little Brother 7

Other Grandmother 8

Brushing Hair 9

Miriam Arrives in America 10

The Boy Next Door 11

Family Trip, 1956: Cousin Linda's Wedding 12

Miriam's Blue Suit 13

Vertebra 14

Wax 15

Lost 16

Legacy 17

Lucky 18

Moving the Peonies 19

Not Like This, My Father 20

Old Letters 21

Raspberry Patch in Winter 22

Pomegranate 23

Bonnard's Painting: *Nude in the Bath and Small Dog* 24

Raspberries 25

Dinner at My Place 26

Yom Kippur under the Night Sky 27

Yellow

Sunflower, goldfinch, goldenrod, yellow jackets on a ripe peach, fat rendered from a chicken in Grandma's kitchen. Upstairs, I helped Mama add yellow drops to margarine so it looked like butter, brushed baby brother's blond curls. I read my picture book about Dorothy and the yellow brick road, saw *Gentlemen Prefer Blondes* at the drive-in with my parents, learned about Anne Frank, the yellow star.

Later on, I went bananas with *Yellow Submarine* and "Mellow Yellow", drank gin with lemonade—then settled down, planted daffodils, had kids, waited for the school bus, began to see with a jaundiced eye. These days, corn is too yellow, too sweet, watermelon yellow when it should be red, the seeds we loved to spit, gone.

The Open Door

On a round palette crusty as Earth,
Bonnard mixed shades of sunlight,
dense profusion of tree and shrub,
tangle of leaf and color.

Surrounded by gardens, at work in a house
where the view expanded every room,
he took possession of mimosas, purple sky,
orange clouds, the almond tree in flower.

In the dining room, an open door
frames a path through unruly vegetation
to the distant sea. Light floods the table
yellow, heats walls to lavender and red.

Outdoors, a table in an arbor, white cloth
blue in the shade, the meal's remains:
wine bottle, apple, coffee cup,
the napkin still warm from my lap.

Monument Beach

Train station still standing, abandoned,
overlooking the beach where we played
all summer—ghost trains now.

Steam engine's chuff and hiss,
pistons turning giant wheels on rails,
clicketa clack clicketa clack—

we hear them before we see them,
jump up from swimming, from digging
in wet sand, run to our places
along the fence as the train appears,
whistle shrieking stay back stay back.

The engineer waves—we know his face,
he's that close, waving to us, blowing
the whistle again, for us—striped hat,
big smile—we want to be like him,
we want to drive that train.

Class Photo

In preschool, two girls said "No!"
and pushed my hands away
when I stuck my clay snake onto theirs,
so I told Mama and she let me stay home
for the rest of the year, playing marbles
on the sidewalk with Ellie and Harvey,
cowboys and Indians, sing-song games.

I liked going shopping with Grandma,
holding her hand when we walked
to Blue Hill Avenue for a chicken
at the kosher butcher, carrots and celery
at the grocer, her newspaper, *Der Tog*,
at the corner store.

When Ellie and I went to kindergarten,
we had to walk past strange people staring
through a fence. And every day, two boys
jumped out from behind a porch to follow us.
Kiss me, said Ronnie, *or I'll put you on a rocket
to the moon.* I knew that was silly,
but I was scared.

At school, Ellie and I drew pictures,
did puzzles and played house together.
Miss Drowne read us stories and never
scolded anyone, not even Mona, who ate
a crayon and got blue all over her mouth.

Perhaps I was daydreaming
when our class photo was taken. There I am—
in the front row with all the other girls, their hands
folded on their laps, faces composed—
my hands flat, one on each knee,
my brow furrowed.

Was I worried about how I was sitting?
or about the walk home?

My Portion

Friday mornings, Grandma made challah for the Sabbath
with dough risen the night before. She'd give me a lump
to play with, cut the rest in three, roll each piece
into a long rope.

I rolled and poked my dough till it was gray,
while Grandma wove her strands into a fat braid
she patted and pushed into a loaf to bake.

When the challah was cool, she cut me a thick slice,
spread half with jam, half with butter, the way I liked it,
though she thought it odd.

I was her "sheyne meydele"—her pretty little girl—
her "zisse kinde"—her sweet child. In her home,
one flight down from ours, I could do no wrong.

Little Brother

Squalling infant, too young to play with,
you were the thief who stole my bedroom,
our mother's heart, then my time with friends—
why did *I* have to walk you to kindergarten?

One day after school, I found you sobbing
in your classroom, stern Miss Wellington
insisting you'd stolen another boy's coat.

You ran to me, held fast to my legs
while my hand rubbed your back.
Even I knew a mistake from a theft.

Other Grandmother

Formal in demeanor, smile elusive, my grandmother
could be severe, *thoughtless and inconsiderate*
her judgment when I didn't behave.

                      More often she indulged me,
let me pick the raisins from her fresh-baked rolls,
poke holes in chocolates till I found my favorite,
choose two new dresses when she'd offered one.

At four, I thought she was old—heavy and slow,
gray hair in a bun on her neck. Nights I slept over,
after we dressed for bed, I watched as she pulled out pins
till her hair tumbled down her back like water,
its ripples softening her face.

Brushing one hundred strokes, she wove her hair
into a miraculous braid, lithe and sinuous,
that tickled the backs of her knees.

Brushing Hair

As a baby, I was bald, hairless till I turned one.
Three years later, the camera caught me smiling
under a mass of messy curls, soon cut
to the nape of my neck.

                I was happy at nine,
when I got to let my hair grow long.
But I didn't expect the hated brushing—
sitting on the bed, my mother behind me
working slowly, not always patiently,
undoing knots of matted hair, teasing them
into separate strands, while I said "ouch",
and "ouch" again.

For years, I didn't cut my hair, reveling
in its growth, a suntouched cloak on my back.
But when it reached my waist, it grew no more.

I wanted hair like Rapunzel's—long enough
to reach the ground beneath a high window,
thick and strong enough for a prince to climb.
I imagined Rapunzel brushing her hair for hours,
making it smooth for her lover's soft hands.
I imagined myself with that hair,
that lover, his hands.

Miriam Arrives in America

Halloween, 1952. I was nine, dressed
as the ballerina I dreamed of becoming.

Our newly discovered cousin
had just arrived from Paris, beautiful
as a princess in the fairy tales I loved.
Her story of the war, worse than anything
in Grimm's—the camps, potato-skin soup—
thrilled me. Knowing her made me special.

Of her family, she was the only survivor:
elegant, smiling, ready—I believed—
to live happily ever after.

The Boy Next Door

Chasing your brother in the old wooden boat, secure
in its cradle in our driveway, you fell headlong
against a cleat near the bow, stood up crying,
holding your head, blood running down your face.

My father ran to grab you, cradled you in his arms
as he hurried to the car, sped off to Dr. Krakauer,
a name we kids thought as funny as his buck teeth.

Book open on my lap, I sat silent on the porch,
watching for our car, unwilling to let my mother
hug me.

When you returned, split brow stitched, a hero
for your bravery, we celebrated at Gooch's
with ice cream, safe, for a while.

Family Trip, 1956: Cousin Linda's Wedding

On a sweltering day in August,
we drove from Boston to Washington DC,
damp washcloth on my father's head,
my mother wetting the cloth with water
from our thermos, my brother and I,
seven and twelve, sweating in the back seat,
bored and restless. I was daydreaming
about my cousin—just graduated from college—
imagining her fancy dress, wondering
if the groom was cute.

At a rest stop in Delaware, dark blood
in my underpants. I knew it was my period,
something other girls got, not me. Worried
about staining my clothes, but too embarrassed
to tell, I waited till we arrived, whispered
the news to my mother. She hugged me,
called my aunt, then sent my father to the drugstore,
while I spoke to Linda, who congratulated me
on "becoming a woman".

I was only twelve. I didn't want the whole family
to know. I didn't want to be a woman, only older,
prettier, more popular. More like my cousin—
she was getting married, she was a woman.

Miriam's Blue Suit

Preparing to leave Paris after the war—mother, father,
brother gone—to live with cousins in America,
she went to a well-known couturier, her boss's friend,
who gave her a price she could afford.

She ordered a suit in a classic style: French blue wool,
velvet trim on the collar of the jacket, a garment
to last a lifetime, armor in an unfamiliar world.
She knew the importance of appearances—
fashionable clothing, a good haircut, makeup.

In the camps, rouge she found hidden on a corpse
gave color to her ashen face, made her look healthy
enough to work, helped save her from the ovens.

Vertebra

You and I ate chicken necks back then,
not because they were cheap, but because we loved
their taste, cooked in a soup with thighs and legs,
carrot and celery, onion and dill.

Sucking soft neck meat from crumbling bone,
we found it delicious, the bone's shape fascinating,
complicated—so much detail in a vertebra
half an inch high.

Cleaned with bleach, set upright on a table,
this almost-X resembled a person, feet
planted firmly, arms raised—a round cavity
at the center
               to hold the cord safe—
the spine's strength its intricate coupling,
vertebrae nested against each other.

You modeled the neck bone in clay, drew it
in ink, carved one from the trunk of a maple,
built another of iron pipe, two stories high—
named it for Daedalus, inventor and artist,
who crafted wings of feathers and wax.

Wax

Mother, I'm throwing you out—
the sculpture of your head, that is,
that Dad made before I was born.
Your nose is squashed—it's only wax,
never meant to be permanent, the nose
a handle when Grandma moved it
from piano to shelf to table and back.

It's the piece I took when Grandma left
for the nursing home—no one else wanted it.
I liked the dark brown wax, sticky to the touch,
patina of dust, a whole sheet of it wrapped
around the base of your neck
to make your shoulders.

It moved with me to New Jersey, California,
Canada, where I left it with my abandoned
boyfriend till I found a place of my own.

By then, your nose was horribly misshapen—
flattened against your cheeks as if a boxer
had landed a punch—overshadowing
the rest of the face, still quite lovely,
eyes closed, lips parted, faint marks
of Dad's fingers on your forehead,
where he smoothed the wax,
made you a crown of hair.

Lost

Why do people say we "lost" him when he died?
as if we'd left him on the beach by mistake
like a forgotten flip-flop, after we'd packed up
towels, shovels, sunblock, and somehow overlooked

our husband and father asleep in the sand where we
buried him up to his neck, face covered with a hat
to protect him from sun. If we'd glanced back
from the car before driving home, surely

we'd have noticed the hat, the mound of sand.
We would have missed him later on, when
he didn't show up for dinner, tried to remember
where we'd last seen him—was he still asleep?

taking one last swim? Perhaps we went back
to the beach, searched for his hat, his sunglasses,
even the core of an apple we thought he'd eaten.

We peered into trashcans, sifted through sand,
walked from one end of the beach to the other,
scanning the water, calling his name.

Legacy

With a fine metal stylus, he drew a landscape,
incising the lines into a flat pallet of clay,
a mold for plaster that—poured, hardened,
removed—became the final work,
everything in relief:

blades of grass alive, leaves trembling on a tree,
ridged bark of the trunk—absence cast into
presence, as memory transforms our dead.

Lucky

With shovel and mattock
my father tears at tangled roots,
uses fulcrum and lever
to prize out old shrubs holding fast
where he wants to plant flowers.
He sits to rest.

He knows he's lucky, strong enough
for bear hugs, the children begging
Break my bones, Grandpa, yielding
soft ribs to his crooked embrace.

But younger friends are dying,
grief a bone that's stuck in his throat—
a whistle of pain as he breathes out memories:
fishing in the bay with his brother, the garden
crowded with corn and tomatoes.

Now he fishes alone, grows only those flowers
that tolerate neglect. Groaning, he rises
to appraise the stubborn roots again.

Moving the Peonies

Under a tall spruce, heavy roots
sucking water from compacted dirt,
the peonies—every spring more stunted,
less and less the beauties my mother planted
years ago. Full heads of white petals, fuschia
in the center, their fragrance filled the room
when she brought them indoors.
Now, in autumn, dead leaf stalks
litter the ground.

Working my spade into hardened earth,
I cut a wide circle, push down deep
to spare the roots, carry each plant
to a sunny bed of airy soil. I remember
my mother, her joy in flowers,
her need to take care of others.

Not Like This, My Father

I don't want him to die like this,
gasping for breath.

Peacefully in his sleep
is what I'd planned—

wouldn't I feel less pain
if he felt none?

Who am I kidding—my rib cage
rising and falling with his.

Old Letters

In the seventies and eighties,
we all wrote letters to stay in touch,
especially my mother and his, weekly at least,
friends, sisters, brothers living in other states—
a blizzard of words, lives in flux.

We were moving, buying houses, looking for jobs,
pumping out flooded basements, going back
to school, falling in love, deciding to get married,
having babies, getting divorced, struggling
with demanding children and bosses.

We were happier then, angrier,
more certain, more unsure. Every word
mattered, too important to throw away—
I saved every letter.

Six boxes full—it seems crazy now—
five and dime stationary, lined paper,
picture postcards and plain. As I read,
I remember forgotten pleasures, troubles—
intimacy absent the person.

Did you mean to sound so cold and hostile?
my mother writes. *Dearests*, his mother begins,
*the phlox is blooming, we're looking forward
to your visit.*

Sarah is growing up at an alarming rate,
my now-dead friend tells me, *she is thin,
complicated and moody—*

reading their letters an act of mourning
that sharpens the sense of loss.

Raspberry Patch in Winter

Rising from deep snow, the canes stand spare,
naked—bright calligraphy in late sun.

Their long shadows—delicate, insubstantial—
reach out across the white expanse.

Wind howls, trashcan lids fly, skitter,
bang against the fence.

The canes press against each other,
whisper their song.

Pomegranate

on a white plate, my own still life.
Fruit lavish as a rose colors the room,
pleases my eye.

For weeks I study its odd shape,
angles like cheekbones, skin taut
with the fullness of what's hidden,
the blossom end a tiny crown.

Voluptuous as an odalisque,
this pomegranate, my work of art—
my eye, the medium.

As rosy skin begins to fade and shrivel,
I struggle to fix forever
the exact shade, the particular form.

With my knife, I lay bare the rows
of tiny fruit bright as rubies,
bite into crisp flesh—sweet, acid.

Bonnard's Painting: *Nude in the Bath and Small Dog*

In the bath, she floats, calmed
by warmth, wetness, a sensation

of lift. Around her, violet walls swell,
blue-green tiles ripple. She drifts

like kelp on the open sea, the tub
holding her steady. Its rim, fluid

as water, bulges where her knee
bends. Her rosy legs are flat,

blurred, her head misshapen, torso
too short, her body dissolving in color.

In the foreground, on a pink rug,
a brown dachshund, clear, precise.

Raspberries

Red, fragrant as jam, they cook
on the cane in hot sun. Sweat oils
your arms, your neck as you swing
the mattock, uproot saplings
invading this unruly patch
once tended by my father,

now mine. Overgrown with vines
too tangled, too numerous to count,
the bushes survive, heavy with berries
so ripe they fall at a touch,
dissolve on our tongues.

On a hot day long ago, we drank
gin and lemonade on the beach,
trying to act grown up, hatching
our plan to return to the house
while my parents were gone.

I lift my shovel, chop through
bittersweet's tough root,
stake my claim to blooms,
to fruit, to hard work shared.
Blood of the raspberry
stains our clothes, our lips.

Dinner at My Place

He grabs a bunch of spinach, a chunk of Romano,
a loaf of bread, while I squeeze every avocado
in the store, dig for one soft enough to eat tonight.
Dinner at my place, too soon, not sure it's right,
or where this is going—but I'm too tired to care,
famished after a day's hike, a futile search
for a table in a restaurant—a public place to share
a meal—on a warm June day near the beach.

He walks into my kitchen, easy as if it's his own,
rummages for a knife, whacks off muddy roots,
snags the spinner to wash and dry the greens,
rustles up cucumber, carrots, puts out plates,
bread, butter. I breathe—cut the unripe avocado,
arrange slices one by one, slowly grate the Romano.

Yom Kippur Under the Night Sky

On this eve of the Day of Atonement, it's hard
to feel solemn—the balmy October evening warm
and humid as a summer night, sky a blur of gray,
the moon fuzzy with moisture.

Twelve hundred chairs line the parking lot.
Sitting in the back row, listening to rush hour sounds
from nearby streets, I watch families trickle in,
find seats and friends, catch up on news—children
of all ages and colors, jeans and striped socks,
tutus and leotards, Superman and Alice.
I can't stop smiling.

Intoxicated by the air, the children, the moment,
I think of my two-week-old grandson,
born into a new moon, a new year.

Soon, he and his parents will join me here.
We will chant the words of Kol Nidre, reflect
on forgiveness, this new life without sin.

Additional Acknowledgments

I am indebted to my Boston area critique group—Mary Buchinger, Philip Burnham, and Ruth Chad—for years of helpful feedback, moral support and the example of their own poems. Martha Collins and Fred Marchant critiqued several of these poems at the Joiner Center Workshop and gave me confidence in their merits. Susan Donnelly's insightful response to the first iteration of the chapbook helped me rethink individual poems and the manuscript as a whole. Members of Susan's ongoing workshop provided helpful criticism of several poems. Mary Buchinger's and Kathleen Spivack's edits to individual poems and suggestions for sequence were invaluable. I am grateful to all of you.

Ruth Ann Smullin grew up in inner city and suburban Boston. As an adult, she lived for 34 years in North Carolina, where she began writing poetry seriously with the help of an experienced critique group. She now lives in the Boston area. Her work has been published in *Bagelbard Anthologies, Common Ground Review, Constellations, Crucible (winner of the Sam Ragan Prize), Ibbetson Street, Naugatuck River Review, Plainsongs, Sow's Ear Poetry Review, The Aurorean,* and is forthcoming in *Atlanta Review.*

www.ingramcontent.com/pod-product-compliance
Lightning Source LLC
LaVergne TN
LVHW041517070426
835507LV00012B/1647